PO

David Adam is the Vicar ⟨...⟩ ministering to thousands o⟨...⟩ born in Alnwick, Northumberland, and was a ⟨...⟩ being ordained. During more than twenty years as Vicar of Danby in North Yorkshire he discovered a gift for composing prayers in the Celtic pattern. Since 1985 he has published four very popular collections of prayers and meditations based on the Celtic tradition, using material he has tried and tested with groups and individuals from his own parishes and on retreat.

Other books by David Adam published by Triangle

THE EDGE OF GLORY
Prayers in the Celtic Tradition 1985

THE CRY OF THE DEER
Meditations on the Hymn of St Patrick 1987

TIDES AND SEASONS
Modern Prayers in the Celtic Tradition 1989

THE EYE OF THE EAGLE
Meditations on the Hymn 'Be thou my vision' 1990

BORDER LANDS
The best of David Adam 1991 (SPCK hardback)

FIRE OF THE NORTH
The Illustrated Life of St Cuthbert 1993 (SPCK)

THE OPEN GATE
Celtic Prayers for Growing Spiritually 1994

THE RHYTHM OF LIFE
Celtic Christian Prayer 1996

FLAME IN MY HEART
St Aidan for Today 1997

POWER LINES

Celtic Prayers about Work

DAVID ADAM

TRIANGLE

First published 1992
Triangle
SPCK
Holy Trinity Church
Marylebone Road
London NW1 4DU

Third impression 1997

British Library Cataloguing in Publication Data
A catalogue record for this book is available from the British Library
ISBN 0-281-04615-8

Photoset by Rowland Phototypesetting Ltd,
Bury St Edmunds, Suffolk
Printed in Great Britain by
Caledonian International Book Manufacturing Ltd, Glasgow

To Dawn and Sharon
and all who love the world

ACKNOWLEDGEMENTS

I would like to thank Jean Freer whose drawings in this book have been an inspiration in themselves. Through her work, Jean has sought to express the mysterious unity of creation, and the Presence in which we dwell.

Thanks also to Jill Patterson and Jim Wightman, both from Holy Island, for their contributions to the art work. I know I am fortunate to have such talent about me.

Will Taylor's cover not only complements the work but in many ways inspired it. These powerful pipe lines, with their interwoven complexities, speak of the powers that flow through us all. I am grateful for such a friend.

I would like to thank David Arthur who floated some of the early ideas with me, whilst he was the National Secretary of the Industrial Christian Fellowship. He shared with me the first thoughts on Power Lines and has remained a hidden support.

Then my thanks to the countless people who have 'endured' my experiments in prayer and meditation, for they have, in fact, made *Power Lines* possible.

The following from Prayers by Others were used with the permission of:
Oxford University Press, for the prayer by John Baillie from *A Diary of Private Prayer* (1936);
Editions du Seuil for the two extracts from *Hymn of the Universe* by Teilhard de Chardin (Fontana 1970);
Lord Runcie of Cuddesdon for his prayer from *Praying With the English Tradition* compiled by Margaret Pawley (Triangle/SPCK 1990);
W & R Chambers Ltd for the prayer from *Hebridean Altars* by Alistair Maclean (1937).

Contents

———

Introduction

When I arrived at a new parish on the North Yorks Moors in the mid-sixties, many people remembered the coming of electricity to those moorland dales. One house still did not have it because the owners refused to have the power lines on their land. They made their choice and excluded themselves. Another elderly lady got the electricity into her house but when the meter was read, the amount used was infinitesimally small. She assured the meter man that she used the electricity every day. A new meter was installed, but with much the same results; there was obviously nothing wrong with the readings. It was in conversation with her that the secret came out: 'Why, I use it every night, and sometimes in the middle of the night. It is the most useful thing to have when you come into the house in the dark. You can put it on until you light your candles.' It was a story told again and again with much laughter, but I realised slowly that this is what we all do. We either refuse to allow the great power of God to come into our lives and homes, or we use the power of the Presence to light our own small candles and then switch off again.

We need to learn to tune in to the Presence that is always there, to become more aware of the power and the peace that is always available and offered to us. In the words of the writer to the Ephesians, we need to 'be strong in the Lord and in the power of His might' (6.10), to discover that it is His strength, His might, and that all power comes from Him. We need to make our own personal discovery that our God is at hand, and He comes in all His power.

Though we may feel that we are alone and in the dark we never are, nor are we left without power. Even when all our human resources seem to have forsaken us, He never leaves us or forsakes us. Throughout each day we need to tune in, to open ourselves to the power of the Presence. We need to learn that we are not that power, that in fact 'we have no power of ourselves to help ourselves', but that such power belongs to God, the Almighty.

We need to discover that, because He is always there; His power flows through His world and through us. It is in that power that we live and move and have our being. We have to re-educate ourselves, to teach ourselves about the Presence and the power of God. We must make our lives accept what we say we assent to, and we must affirm our belief through our actions and reactions. It is no use preaching a gospel of love if we go around hating people; it is no use talking about an Almighty God if we believe that we are beyond his help or care.

This is not positive thinking, it is far more than that. It is seeking to extend our sensitivities, our awareness, our vision, to experience the reality of His Presence. We need to give body to the words we say, so that they have meaning. Recently someone told me that they found a Communion service boring. Now I do not doubt that I can be boring, but communion with God cannot be boring. I asked them to look with me at the opening words, 'The Lord is here. His Spirit is with us.' That fact cannot be boring even if our response to it is. Much of this book is an attempt to re-tune ourselves so that we may vibrate to the Presence, to help us affirm in our lives what we say we believe. For us all, this will mean taking time to peel away the layers of insensitivity and trivia which we have woven around ourselves, so that we may become alert and alive to what shapes our lives, and become aware of Who is with us. I believe this will be harder for those who are city dwellers, by the very nature of their surroundings. It is not that God has left the city, it is that it offers so many places to escape and to hide ourselves from Him. There are more layers in the city to peel away in order to discover the Divine Milieu. Yet this is a great adventure in itself. This is for us our pilgrimage of love.

Another image from the North Yorks Moors comes from the water supply, gained from fresh moorland springs. This was beautiful soft peaty water, but with it came tiny grains of peat or sand. Slowly but surely these grains desposited themselves at a low point in the pipeline, until after months or years, suddenly the water ceased to flow. The water was there, the reservoir was full, there was even water in the pipe. But, it was dammed (emotive word) and so it could not flow. It was as if it had been turned off. There are so many people like this, full of potential, with loads of ability, with the very Presence about them, but they are blocked off. With a blocked pipe there is no use plodding on in hope, we must unblock it. While it is dammed, it is useless, so it must be set free. So with ourselves; we need to be freed to experience 'the glorious liberty of the children of God'. Some of the prayers in this book seek to do that for us, to unblock our ears and to open our eyes to the Presence and the power that is all about us.

I believe in recital theology. The best way to learn of the Presence is to hammer it home – not to convince ourselves but to open ourselves. This is not auto-suggestion; it is something far richer than that. But it is like hammering a nail into a piece of wood. It is very unlikely that you will be able to do it in one blow. It will take many blows to drive it home. Refrains in prayer are good to use so long as they are used to drive the truth deeper, or to drive the reality into our awareness. I watched a pile driver in the city driving deeply into the foundations great girders to undergird the building that would be built above, and I knew that was what I was seeking to do in some of my prayers, I wanted them to undergird the very structure of my life. I wanted these prayers to be allowed to become so much part of my daily living that whatever happened, from Him (not from the prayers) I would find power and stability.

When there is so much upheaval going on in our lives, we need to have firm foundations. The industries of our land, the cities and their structures are all being shaken in one way or another, and we need to know where there is secure ground, if there is any. We have to discover the God who is the ground of our being, the firm foundation, the power that is not dependent on us or on earthly manipulations. That power is there, and waits to be discovered through the opening of our sensitivities and through our prayer.

Much of Celtic prayer spoke naturally to God in the working place of life. There was no false division into sacred and secular. God pervaded all and was to be met in their daily work and travels. If our God is to be found only in our churches and our private prayers, we are denuding the world of His reality and our faith of credibility. We need to reveal that our God is in all the world and waits to be discovered there – or, to be more exact, the world is in Him, all is in the heart of God. Our work, our travels, our joys and our sorrows are enfolded in his loving care. We cannot for a moment fall out of the hands of God. Typing pool and workshop, office and factory are all as sacred as the church. The Presence of God pervades the work place as much as He does a church sanctuary.

This should provide us with confidence and hope. This is the source of all power, and in His love he makes Himself available in our offices and shops, in our factories and industries. Our God is not a god who is afar off, He has not left us totally to our own devices; though He has given us the freedom to ignore Him if we so choose. Yet the words of St John still ring true: 'As many as receive him to them He gives the power to become sons and daughters of God.' The Power lines are always open and they are available to you.

The Power lines weave through our world, through our society, through creation itself. There is no place where they are not available, no place where He is not present. Great resources are made available to us at all times, and we tend to choose to remain like paupers. The light is offered and we have elected to stay in the dark. Yet the Power lines, the personal Presence, remains and waits, that we may open our lives to Him and discover the glorious liberty of the children of God. Seek to open your heart and your life to Him. Discover that 'in Him we live and move and have our being.'

MORNING

Shine on Me

As the sun rises, Lord,
Let your light shine on me.
Destroy the darkness about me,
Scatter the darkness before me,
Disperse the darkness behind me,
Dispel the darkness within me.
Let your light shine on me.

As the sun rises, Lord,
Let your light shine on me.
The warmth of your Presence,
The brightness of your love,
The radiance of your joy,
The shining of your hope.
Let your light shine on me.

As the sun rises, Lord,
Let your light shine on me.
Your light to guide,
Your light to lead,
Your light to direct,
Your light to brighten.
Let your light shine on me.

Waken Me, O Lord

Waken me, O Lord,
> Open my eyes to your glory
> Open my ears to your story
> Open my heart to your fire
> Open my will to your desire.

Waken me, O Lord,
> To your risen power
> To your Presence every hour
> To your never-ending love
> To your coming from above.

Waken me, O Lord,
> To your peace here today
> To your meeting in the way
> To your speaking in a friend
> To your guiding to the end.

Waken me, O Lord, to your glory.

Lord, Open My Eyes

Lord, open my eyes
That I sleep not in death.

Open my eyes
To your glory about me.

Open my eyes
That I may perceive wonders.

Open my eyes
To look deep into mysteries.

Open my eyes
That I walk not in darkness.

For all who awaken
See infinite treasures
And find you in the city.
All who awaken
See marvels untold
And life in Infinity.

Help Me, Lord

Help me, Lord, to see
You are about me.
You are my hope.

In my lying down and rising
In my travelling and arriving
    Help me, Lord, to see
    You are about me.
    You are my hope.

In my sorrow and enjoyment
In my work and unemployment
    Help me, Lord, to see
    You are about me.
    You are my hope.

In my health and in my sickness
In my strength and in my weakness
    Help me, Lord, to see
    You are about me.
    You are my hope.

In my peacefulness and strife
In my going from this life
    Help me, Lord, to see
    You are about me.
    You are my hope.

In my achievement and its waning
In my losing or my gaining
        Help me, Lord, to see
        You are about me.
        You are my hope.

The final word may be changed from HOPE to PEACE,
LIFE, or whatever we feel we need to flow from the
Presence.

Morning Dedication

In all I do this day,
In all I think or say,
Father, be with me all the way.

In all my work and all my deeds,
In all I learn, in all my needs,
Christ, go before me, the One who leads.

In my work as I do my best,
In all that puts me to the test,
Spirit, help, and grant me rest.

Openings

O Lord God, Creator of all
Open my eyes to beauty
Open my mind to wonder
Open my ears to others
Open my heart to you.

Adoration

Father,
      In you is my birth,
      In you is the earth,
      In you is eternal worth.
            I bow before you.

Jesus,
      In you is love so dear,
      In you salvation near,
      In you I lose my fear.
            I bow before you.

Spirit,
      In you is all strong power,
      In you is every hour,
      In you my life will flower.
            I bow before you.

Affirmations

I believe, O God, that you are
The Eternal Father of peace
The Eternal Father of power
The Eternal Father of all people.

I believe, O God, that you are
The Lord and giver of longings
The Lord and giver of life
The Lord and giver of love.

I believe, O God, that you are
The Spirit of all glory
The Spirit of all goodness
The Spirit of all grace.

I believe, O God, that you are
Here and with me now.

God is with me
God beside me
God to protect me
God to guide me
God to enfold me
God to heal me
God to uphold me
God to restore me.

The Peace of the Presence

I believe, O God of all gods,
that you are present,
that we dwell in you
and in your Presence there is Peace.

I believe, O God of all gods,
that you are present,
that this day begins in you
and in your Presence there is Peace.

I believe, O God of all gods,
that you are present,
that this journey is in you
and in your Presence there is Peace.

I believe, O God of all gods,
that you are present,
that this work place is in you
and in your Presence there is Peace.

I believe, O God of all gods,
that you are present,
that we dwell in you
and in your Presence there is Peace.

This prayer of affirmation is easily learned by heart. Three lines remain constant. The third line seeks to affirm the reality in the particular, such as office, shop, railway station. The very last word can be changed from peace to love, joy, light, hope, or whatever quality you feel you lack and which is found in the Presence.

The Deep Peace of God

Peace, Lord, peace.
Help me, by your peace
To give peace
To radiate peace
To receive peace
To achieve peace.
Teach me, by your peace
When to forgo peace
When to disturb peace
When to distil peace
Always to be at peace
O Lord God of Peace.

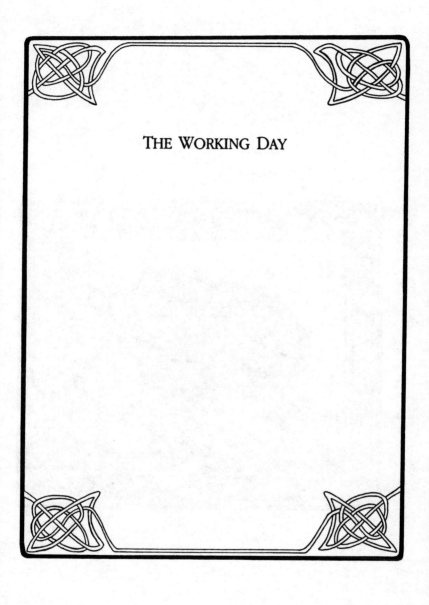

THE WORKING DAY

Dedication

I give my work to you, Lord.
I give my work to you.

I give my plans to you, Lord.
I give my plans to you.

I give my hopes to you, Lord.
I give my hopes to you.

I give my dreams to you, Lord.
I give my dreams to you.

I give my life to you, Lord.
I give my life to you.

I give my love to you, Lord.
I give my love to you.

Keep me true to you, Lord.
Keep me true to you.

In all I say and do, Lord,
In all I say and do.

Help me to serve you, Lord.
Help me to serve you.

Lord, Whatever . . .

Lord,
Whatever we build,
Give us a glimpse of glory.
Whatever we make,
Give us a sense of wonder.
Wherever we travel,
Give us a sense of reverence.
Whoever we meet,
Give us a sense of awe.
Whatever we do,
Give us a sense of achievement.
Whatever our situation,
Give us knowledge of you.

Help us to see that everything is in your care
And that you allow us to share in your glory.

Mighty God

Mighty God,
Holy and strong One,
Give us strength
To do what you would have us do.
Deliver us from lack of purpose,
Free us from confusion of mind,
Save us from loss of integrity,
Maintain in us vision and ideals,
Sustain our openness and generosity.
Help us to continue to work for you,
That we may serve you all our days,
Mighty God,
Holy and strong One.

Enable Us, O God

Enable us, Father, Creator,
To walk in your light
To work by your might
To long for your sight.

Enable us, Jesus, Redeemer,
To look for your healing
To know your appealing
To live for your revealing.

Enable us, Spirit, Strengthener,
With power through your confiding
With peace through your providing
With Presence through your abiding.

Enable us,
Trinity
In Unity,
Unity
In Trinity.
Enable us, O God.

Make Me Aware

Make me aware, O Lord,

of the eye that beholds me
   the hand that holds me
   the heart that loves me
   the Presence that enfolds me.

Power to Work

Lord you are
The love of my life
The light of my way
The peace of my mind
The power for my task
The Presence

Help me
Strong One
To be a strength to the weak
Help me
Caring One
To be a support to the sad
Help me
Saving One
To be a helper of the lost
Help me
Present One
To be a comfort to the lonely
Help me
Holy One
To worship you now and evermore

Prayer for Another

As runs the river down to the sea
May God's love to you flow free.
As lap the waves upon the shore
God's Presence come to you evermore.
As mighty hills rise in their place
May God fill you with His good grace.
As streams in valleys run so deep
May God's strong arm protect and keep.
As shines the sun so faithfully
May God give His prosperity.
As God Most High created you
May He fill your whole life through.
As Christ the Saviour hung on cross
May He redeem your life from loss.
As the Spirit shall on you descend
May He become your lasting friend.
As you are surrounded by the Trinity
May they protect you unto infinity.

Lord of All

Lord of all,
You made us for yourself
And for your great glory.
Bless us, body and soul,
Shield us, keep us whole.
Bless all our intention
By your intervention.
Bless our words and all our deeds,
Guide us where our action leads.
Bless the workings of our mind,
Make us sensitive and kind.
Make us gentle in our dealings,
Bless our hearts with finer feelings.
Fill our lives with joyous laughter
And with glory ever after.

Teach me, Lord,
to give
of my time
my talents
my trust
myself.
Help me, Lord,
to receive
from others,
to delegate,
to share,
and in all to be aware of you.

Vision

O Lord,
Extend our vision,
Our clearness of sight.
Open our eyes to see
Beyond the obvious,
To perceive that this is your world.
You are in it,
You invade it,
You pervade it,
You enfold it,
It is immersed in you.
Here we encounter you,
Here we meet you,
Here you come to us,
Here your presence waits to be revealed.

O Lord,
Extend our vision,
Our clearness of sight.
Open our eyes to see
In the depth of reality,
Your grace,
Your goodness,
Your glory,
To see that we dwell in you,
That you are in us,
That you are with us always.
Here you offer us your kingdom.

Life-giver

You are the Lord,
The giver of life.
You are the Lord,
Protector from strife.
You are the Lord
With me today.
You are the Lord
Guiding my way.
You are the Lord,
Almighty and King.
You are the Lord,
Accept what I bring.

THE CITY

Fleeting Presence

In the crowded street,
On the commuter train,
I saw His Presence there.

In the news flash,
In the bleak rain,
Was God, beyond compare.

Caught up in commerce,
In the superstore,
I saw Him once again.

In the car crash,
With the homeless,
Was God, who shares our pain.

At my wits' end,
In the rush hour,
Was God, who keeps me sane.

Unexpected, uninvited,
Long ignored and long rejected,
He will come again.

Escalator Prayer

As I ascend this stair
I pray for all who are in despair.

All who have been betrayed
All who are dismayed
All who are distressed
All who feel depressed
All ill and in pain
All who are driven insane
All whose hope has flown
All who are alone
All homeless on the street
All who with danger meet.

Lord, who came down to share our plight,
Lift them into your love and light.

Silence Us, That We May Hear

Amid the crowds that clamour,
Amid the demands that call,
Amid the things that shout,
Silence us, that we may hear.

Amid the ceaseless rounds,
Amid the hurried pace,
Amid the countless journeys,
Silence us, that we may hear.

Amid the hasty thoughts,
Amid the speedy reactions,
Amid the swift communications,
Silence us, that we may hear.

Amid the powers that threaten,
Amid the people who manipulate,
Amid the robbers of our freedom,
Silence us, that we may hear.

Amid all our fellow workers,
Amid all our leisure-sharers,
Amid all our homes and families,
Silence us, that we may hear.

Traveller's Prayers

In our journeying this day,
Keep us, Father, in your way.
In seeking of a vision true,
Keep us, Saviour, close to you.
In our desire to do your will,
Keep us, Spirit, guide us still.
In our striving to be free,
Keep and help us, Blest Trinity.

In your journey by land, air or sea,
God's almighty hand protecting be.
May He be your strength and shield,
Whether in commerce, city or field.
In busy office, or crowded street,
May the Wisdom of God guide your feet.

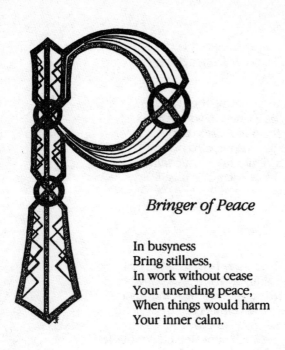

Bringer of Peace

In busyness
Bring stillness,
In work without cease
Your unending peace,
When things would harm
Your inner calm.

Invitations

Come, God of Peace
Come, God of Above
Come, Lord of Life
Come, Lord of Love
Come, Spirit of Hope
Come, most Holy Dove
Come now,
Come in this stranger.

God Bless the Earth

God bless the earth
And all living creatures
God bless the earth
With its rugged features
God bless the earth
Every town and city
God bless the earth
With all its industry
God bless the earth
Atmosphere and air
God bless the earth
Keep it in your care
God bless the earth
Protect the living soil
God bless the earth
May nothing despoil
God bless the earth
And its daily light
God bless the earth
Preserve it by your might.

Invocation

On all of creation,
The animate and inanimate,
The weak and the strong,
The young and the old,
The wise and the simple,
The free and the captive,
The peaceful and the anxious,
The joyful and the sad,
The saint and the sinner,
The living and the dead,
Be the grace and glory of God.

Thy Kingdom Come

Come, Lord Jesus,
Come as King.

Rule in our hearts,
Come as love.

Rule in our minds,
Come as peace.

Rule in our actions,
Come as power.

Rule in our days,
Come as joy.

Rule in our darkness,
Come as light.

Rule in our bodies,
Come as health.

Rule in our labours,
Come as hope.

Thy Kingdom come
Among us.

The first or the last couplet may be used after every
sentence.

Revelations

Lord,
Reveal in us your glory
Stir in us your power
Open in us your love
Work in us your miracles
Show in us your way
Renew in us your kingdom
Abide in us Yourself.

ACHIEVEMENT

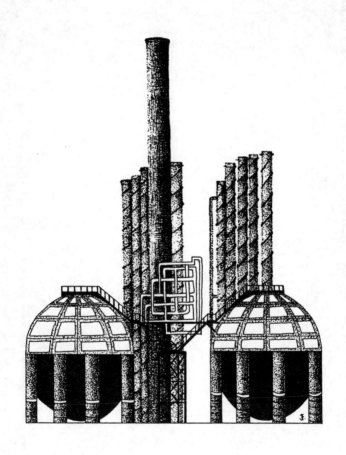

Beyond Ourselves

Grant us a vision, Lord,
To see what we can achieve
To reach out beyond ourselves
To share our lives with others
To stretch our capabilities
To increase our sense of purpose
To be aware of where we can help
To be sensitive to your Presence
To give heed to your constant call.

Thanksgiving

For the potential you have given us
For the possibilities that lie before us
We thank you, heavenly Father.

For our plans and their fulfilment
For your promises and their enjoyment
We thank you, heavenly Father.

In the problems that await us
In the perils that will meet us
Protect us, Heavenly Father.

In the pains of our achievements
In the powers that would control us
Protect us, heavenly Father.

In our purposes and leisure
In our passions and our pleasure
Protect us, heavenly Father.

In the Power of God

In all I think, or do, or say,
In all that I achieve today,
Let it be in the Father's way.

In my working, in seeking right,
Until the coming of the night,
Let it be in the Saviour's might.

In my actions, in every place,
In my running of the race,
Let it be in the Spirit's grace.

In my travelling to the city,
In my deeds of love and pity,
Guide me, ever most Holy Trinity.

God of love and gentleness
Keep us by your great goodness
From each act of sinfulness
From each deed of carelessness
From each word of hurtfulness
From each thought of evilness
Keep, O Lord, and ever bless
With your peace and holiness
God of love and gentleness.

With All My Senses

I pray with my mind
To be sensitive, kind
I pray with my heart
To be loving each part
I pray with each deed
To God may they lead
I pray with my will
Your Presence instil
I pray all my days
I fill them with praise.

Bless, O Father, all that I behold
Bless, O Father, all in speech told
Bless, O Father, all that I hear
Bless, O Jesus, each feeling dear.
Bless, O Jesus, all that I smell
Bless, O Jesus, each taste as well.
Bless, O Spirit, all of each art
Bless, O Spirit, Love of my heart,
Bless, O Spirit, all that is real
Bless, O Trinity, with love seal.

Christ is

Christ, the Good Shepherd, seek
All who are lost, all who are weak.
Christ, Israel's fruitful Vine,
Around each heart your love entwine.
Christ, the Gateway and the Door,
Give us life for evermore.
Christ, the Water flowing free,
Refresh us for eternity.
Christ, show us yourself the Way,
That we may follow you alway.
Christ, may we see in you the Light,
Banish from us the dreadful night.
Christ, feed us, Jesus Christ the Bread,
That you may raise us from the dead.
Christ, Resurrection for all to see,
Surround us through eternity.

God of Life

Lord increase
My zest for living
My vision of glory
My hearing of your call
My grasp on reality
My response to your love
My sensitivity to others
My gentleness to creation
My taste for wonder
My love for you.

DISAPPOINTMENT

The Vision of God

Lord, my vision is dull,
Lord, my heart is weary,
my will is weak;
Open my eyes to your glory,
Renew my heart with your love,
Strengthen my will with your purpose
and make me aware of you,
You indwelling,
You abiding.
You are in this city,
All things reside in you.

You are great, the Mighty One
You are the Most High,
You are the Creator,
Maker of heaven and earth.
You sustain all,
You love all,
You enfold all,
Lord God, Holy One.
You are our peace,
You are our joy,
You are our hope,
You are our light,
You are our life,
You are our eternal future.
Holy God,
Holy and strong One,
You are found in our midst,
With us now
And for evermore.

Enfold Me

Lord, enfold me,
In the depths of your love
and there hold me.
Renew my being,
Refine, refresh, restore me.
Raise me up and remould me,
Until my whole being is aglow
With your glory and goodness,
Gracious and generous God.

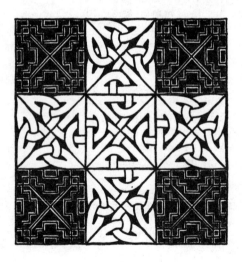

Vibrations

When the days are heavy
And my strength is small
Let my heart vibrate
With your constant call.
Let me know that it is true
I am loved and belong to you.

When life is weary
And friends seem few,
Give me your power,
My strength renew.

When friends are many
And life is full,
Give me clear vision,
Let me not be dull.

When all is over,
And action is past,
Reveal your Presence,
Bring me home at last.

The Furnace of God's Love

Lord, I am poured out,
I come to you for renewal.
Lord, I am weary,
I come to you for refreshment.
Lord, I am worn,
I come to you for restoration.
Lord, I am lost,
I come to you for guidance.
Lord, I am troubled,
I come to you for peace.
Lord, I am lonely,
I come to you for love.
Come, Lord,
Come revive me
Come re-shape me
Come mould me in your image.
Re-cast me in the furnace of your love.

One in Him

Lord, I am disturbed
I am distressed
I am divided
I am disgusted.
I come to you for healing
I come to you for peace
I come to you for restoring
I come to you for dignity.

Help me, Lord,
To do what you would have me do,
To become the person you want me to be.

Healing God

Weary and worn
In want and woe
We wish for you
We watch for you
We wait for you.
Holy God
Holy and Strong One
Holy and Immortal One
Have mercy upon us.

Come Mighty God
Come without delay
Come as our helper
Come as our way
Come as our Saviour
Come Lord we pray
Come as our healer
Come Lord today.

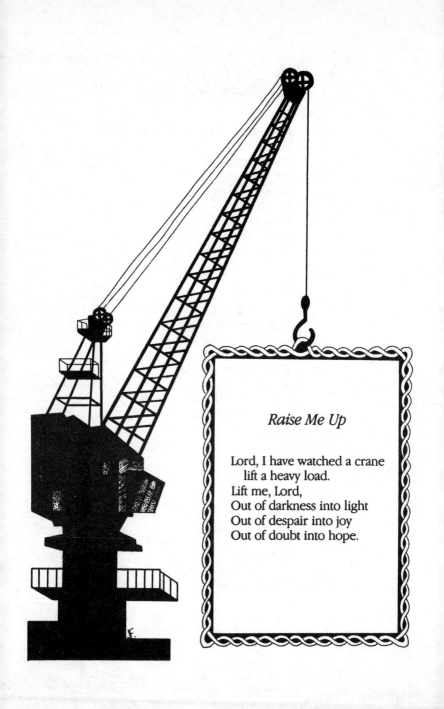

Raise Me Up

Lord, I have watched a crane
  lift a heavy load.
Lift me, Lord,
Out of darkness into light
Out of despair into joy
Out of doubt into hope.

Raise Me Up

Lord, I have watched a crane lift a heavy load.
Lift me, Lord,
Out of darkness into light
Out of despair into joy
Out of doubt into hope.

Lift me, Lord,
Out of sadness into laughter
Out of sickness into health
Out of shadows into light.

Lift me, Lord,
Out of fear into hope
Out of frailty into strength
Out of foolishness into sense.

Lift me, Lord.
You came down to lift us
You descended to hell to lift us to heaven
You entered death to raise us to life.
Come, Lord, raise me up, I pray you.

Wielder of Victories

Father, Creator, of all mankind
Protect my body and soul entwined.

Jesus, risen in glorious light.
Lift me out of the darkest night.

Spirit, life-giver, keep me whole,
Healthy in body, mind, and soul.

Trinity, safety and protection still,
Keep me from all harm and ill.

Unity, watch me with your eye,
Let your hand be ever nigh.

Almighty, shield me by your power,
God be with me every hour.

Wielder of Victories, all praise to you,
Father, Son and the Spirit so true.

The Comforter

Comforter of the weak
All the lost you seek
Be sight to the blind
Restore the sick in mind
Be joy to all the sad
A calming to the mad
To all who are alone
Make your Presence known
The disappointed cheer
Showing you are near
All in every plight
Protect with your might
Bring us to the dawn
Of Resurrection morn
That we may joyful be
In your bright eternity

Lord, Come Down

Lord Jesus Christ, who did descend
To become a sinner's friend,
Heal our wounds and soothe our sorrow
Help us face a new tomorrow.
Reach into our darkest deep,
Lift us up and safely keep.
Save us from our body's pain,
Give us that full life again.
Lord Jesus Christ, who did descend,
Protect and aid us to the end.

Shape Me, O God

Lord, I am poured out like water,
Emptied like a hollowed drum.
I am wrung out to the last drop.

Now there is more room for you.
Mould me and shape as you will,
Direct the way my life should flow.

Come, fill my whole being with glory.
Pour into me your great power,
Saturate me with your goodness.

De Profundis

Out of the deep I call, O God,
Out of the dark of my own night,
Out of the deep I call, O God,
Lord, come in your great might.

Out of the deep I call, O God,
Out of the depth of my despair,
Out of the deep I call, O God,
Lord, come, lift me from there.

Out of the deep I call, O God,
Out of the turmoil of my soul,
Out of the deep, I call, O God,
Lord, come, and make me whole.

Out of the deep I call, O God,
Out of the agony of my being,
Out of the deep I call, O God,
Lord, come, my whole life freeing.

God, who brought me to this night,
Hold me fast by your great might.
God, lead me to another shore.
God, help me praise you evermore.
God, guide me over the last great sea.
God, grant me the haven of eternity.

Glory Through and Through

Though the way is weary
And the future seems dreary
Though my strength is weak
And I have passed my peak
There is a song in my soul
For I have an eternal goal
I know that I belong to you
That glory fills me through and through.

EVENING

Light of the World

Light of the world,
Enter into the depths
   of our lives.

Come into the dark
   and hidden places.

Walk in the storehouse
   of our memories.

Hear the hidden secrets
   of the past.

Plumb the very depth
   of our being.

Be present through
   the silent hours,

And bring us safely
   to your glorious light.

Commendation

I rest in your love
Father above
I rest in your peace
Let it not cease
I rest in your joy
Let nothing destroy
I rest in your might
Keep me this night
I rest in your grace
Protect this my place.

The Hand of God

The waves roar, the winds increase;
Lift me up, Lord, to your peace.
The way is dark, the night is cold;
Keep me safe, Lord, in your hold.
My faith is weak, my vision dim;
Save me Lord, I cannot swim.
Let your hand reach down to me,
Lift me from my perplexity.
Let your powerful, mighty hand
Bring me safe again to land.

Possess me, Lord

Lord,
Let me seek
Not so much to possess as to be possessed.
Not so much to grasp as to be grasped.
Not so much to own as to be owned.
For you gave yourself
As a ransom for many
And taught
It is more blessed to give
than to receive.
Come, take me, Lord.
Come, I am yours.
Come, possess me now.

Protection

The storms rage about me,
Keep them, Lord, without me.
Troubles would confound me,
Let them not surround me.
Evil would ensnare me,
Let it not come near me.
Calm the wind,
Make the waves cease,
Enfold me Lord,
In your peace.

Give me a Vision

Give me a vision, that I may see
Almighty God in His majesty.
Give me a faith, that I may trust
Jesus my Saviour, risen from dust.
Give me a love, that I may feel
The Holy Spirit close and real.
Give me a loyalty, that I may be
Rejoicing forever in the Trinity.

Eternal God

Eternal love
Come from above.

Eternal light
Shatter our night.

Eternal hope
Help us to cope.

Eternal peace
Bring us release.

Eternal might
Be at our right.

Eternal Three
Ever with me.

Eternal, abide
Close at my side.

Eternal, Infinity,
Protect this your city.

Evening Dedication

Here are my thoughts, Lord,
Here is my mind.
Here are my deeds, Lord,
Help me unwind.

Here is my strength, Lord,
Here is my will.
Here is my life, Lord,
Help me be still.

Here is my heart, Lord,
Here is my hope.
Here is my love, Lord,
Help me to cope.

Here is my time, Lord,
Here is my might,
Here I am thine, Lord,
Bless me tonight.

Shielding of God

The Saviour to shield
Your house and home
The Saviour to shield
Where'er you roam
The Saviour to shield
In darkest hour
The Saviour to shield
By his mighty power
The Saviour to shield
When facing defeat
The Saviour to shield
In the troubled street
The Saviour to shield
At every turn
The Saviour to shield
And show His concern
The Saviour to shield
Today and tomorrow
The Saviour to shield
And keep you from sorrow.

Lighten Our Darkness

Lighten our darkness,
Lord, we pray.
Lighten our darkness
At the end of the day.
Defend us from danger
And perils this night
For the love of Jesus
The Lord who is Light.

Lighten our burden,
Lord, we ask.
Lighten our burden
Bring joy to our task.
Give peace in our labour
To work bring your might
For the love of Jesus
The Lord who is Light.

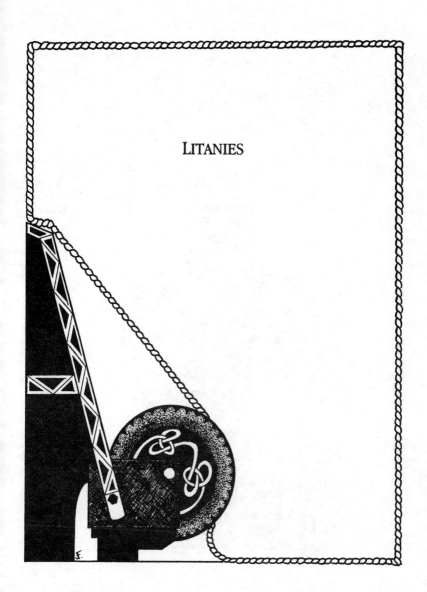

LITANIES

Thy Kingdom Come

In the quiet of the morning,
In the new day that is dawning,
Thy Kingdom come.

In my waking and my dressing,
In my life and its progressing,
Thy Kingdom come.

In this moment for the taking,
In the things that I am making,
Thy Kingdom come.

In the people I am meeting,
In each one I shall be greeting,
Thy Kingdom come.

In my tasks and my employment,
In my leisure and enjoyment,
Thy Kingdom come.

All day, until its very ending,
Praise to you I shall be sending,
Thy Kingdom come.

O Lord, Forgive and Give

For our insensitivity to your creation,
For vandalism and violence,
For crassness and carelessness,
Forgive us, O Lord.

For hardness and hatred,
For cruelty and callousness,
Forgive us, O Lord.

For baseness and blindness,
For rebellion and ruthlessness,
Forgive us, O Lord.

For greed and gracelessness,
For indifference and ignorance,
Forgive us, O Lord.

For disrespect and drabness,
For lack of sense and laziness,
Forgive us, O Lord.

Grace and goodness,
Love and liveliness,
Give us, O Lord.

Calm and carefulness,
Generosity and goodness,
Give us, O Lord.

Peace and prosperity,
Hope and healthiness,
Give us, O Lord.

Strength and security,
Employment and enjoyment,
Give us, O Lord.

Inner Longings

Lord of this world
We work
We watch
We wait for you.
Come down
Come in
Come among us.

Lord of this life
We labour
We look
We long for you.
Come down
Come in
Come among us.

Lord of this second
We strive
We serve
We search for you.
Come down
Come in
Come among us.

That we may dwell in you
And you in us
For ever.

A Voice in the Night

Father Almighty, Lord of all,
Hear your loved one when I call.

Jesus all loving, Saviour of all,
Hear your loved one when I call.

Spirit all Powerful, guide of all,
Hear your loved one when I call.

Trinity all blessed, ruler of all,
Hear your loved one when I call.

Peace, Lord, Peace.
To all whom I meet
To all in the street
Peace, Lord, Peace.

To all working here
To all who are dear
Peace, Lord, Peace.

To all who need pity
To all in this city
Peace, Lord, Peace.

To all facing defeat
Who feel incomplete
Peace, Lord, Peace.

To all unemployed
Whose hope is destroyed
Peace, Lord, Peace.

To all who lack mirth
To all the wide earth
Peace, Lord, Peace.

To all who need grace
To us in this place
Peace, Lord, Peace.

Come, Creator, Come

From chaos and emptiness
From loneliness and lifelessness
Come, Creator, come.

From darkness and shapelessness
From the abyss and dreadfulness
Come, Creator, come.

From fearfulness and hopelessness
From weakness and fruitlessness
Come, Creator, come.

Come to your creation
As we wait
and watch
and wish for you.
Come and re-create us in your likeness,
O God, who can create from nothing
And bring order out of chaos.
Come and re-fashion us in your glory.

Good Lord, Deliver Us

From empty hours
And waning powers
Good Lord, deliver us.

From lack of peace
And mind's disease
Good Lord, deliver us.

From sore disgrace
And lack of face
Good Lord, deliver us.

From darkest night
From taking fright
Good Lord, deliver us.

From feeling tense
From lack of sense
Good Lord, deliver us.

Be with us to protect us
Within us to pacify us
Behind us to defend us
Before us to lead us
Near us to comfort us
Above us to lift us
Beneath us to support us.

PRAYERS BY OTHERS

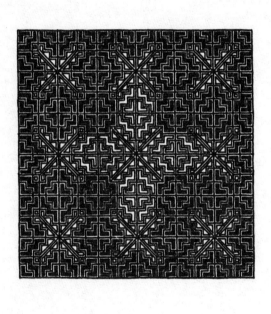

Give us, O Lord,
A steadfast heart,
Which no unworthy thought can drag downwards:
An unconquered heart,
Which no tribulation can wear out;
An upright heart,
Which no unworthy purpose can tempt aside.
Give us, O Lord,
Understanding to know you,
Diligence to seek you,
Wisdom to find you,
And a faithfulness
That may embrace you,
Through Jesus Christ our Lord.

St Thomas Aquinas (1225–74)

O Lord our God,
Who has called us to serve you,
In the midst of the world's affairs,
When we stumble, hold us;
When we fall, lift us up;
When we are hard pressed with evil, deliver us;
When we turn from what is good, turn us back;
And bring us at last to your glory.

Alcuin (*c*. 735–804)

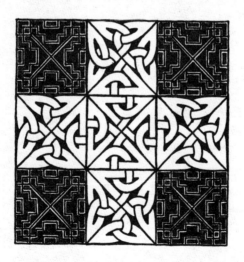

Support us, O Lord,
All the day long of this troublous life,
Until the shades lengthen,
And evening comes,
The busy world is hushed,
The fever of life is over,
And our work here is done.
Then, Lord, in your mercy,
Grant us safe lodging,
A holy rest,
And peace at the last,
Through Jesus Christ our Lord.

The Office of Compline

Lord, make me an instrument of your peace.
Where there is hatred, let me sow love;
Where there is injury, pardon;
Where there is discord, union;
Where there is doubt, faith;
Where there is despair, hope;
Where there is darkness, light;
Where there is sadness, joy;
For your mercy and your truth's sake.

The 'Prayer of St Francis'

God be in my head
And in my understanding
God be in my eyes
And in my looking
God be in my mouth
And in my speaking
God be in my heart
And in my thinking
God be at my end
And at my departing
Anonymous, Medieval

To my God a heart of flame,
To my fellow men a heart of love,
To myself a heart of steel.
St Augustine (354–430)

Lead us from the unreal
to the real.
Lead us from darkness
to light.
Lead us from death
to immortality.
A Prayer from India

God grant me the serenity
to accept the things I cannot change,
the courage to change the things I can,
and the wisdom to know the difference.
Reinhold Niebuhr (1892–1971)

We beg you, Lord,
    to help and defend us.
Deliver the oppressed,
pity the insignificant,
raise the fallen,
show yourself to the needy,
heal the sick,
bring back your people
    who have gone astray,
feed the hungry,
lift up the weak,
take off the prisoner's chains.
May every nation come to know
that you are God.
that Jesus Christ is your Child,
that we are your people,
the sheep of your pasture.
                Clement of Rome (*c.* 200)

O Lord, I remember before thee tonight
all the workers of the world:
Workers with hand or brain;
Workers in cities or in fields;
Men who go forth to toil
and women who keep house;
Employers and employees;
Those who command and those who obey;
Those whose work is dangerous;
Those whose work is monotonous or mean;
Those who can find no work to do;
Those whose work is in the service of the poor
or the healing of the sick
or the proclamation of the Gospel of Christ
At home or in foreign places.

John Baillie (1886–1960)

Dearest Lord, teach me to be generous;
Teach me to serve Thee as Thou deservest;
To give and not to count the cost,
To fight and not to heed the wounds,
To toil and not to seek for rest,
To labour and not to ask for any reward,
Save that of knowing that I do Thy will.

St Ignatius Loyola (1491–1556)

O Lord, Thou knowest how busy I must be this day;
if I forget thee do not Thou forget me:
  for Christ's sake.

General Lord Astley (1578–1652)
before the battle of Edgehill

God in Matter

Glorious Lord Christ: the divine influence secretly diffused and active in the depths of matter, and the dazzling centre where all the innumerable fibres of the manifold meet; power as implacable as the world and as warm as life . . . you whose hands imprison the stars; you who are the first and the last, the living and the dead and the risen again; you who gather into your exuberant unity every beauty, every affinity, every energy, every mode of existence, it is you to whom my being cries out with a desire as vast as the universe, 'In truth you are my Lord and my God.'

Teilhard de Chardin (1881–1955)
'The Mass on the World'

Blessed be you, harsh matter, barren soil, stubborn rock: you who yield only to violence, you who force us to work if we would eat.

Blessed be you, perilous matter, violent sea, untameable passion: you who unless we fetter you will devour us.

Blessed be you, mighty matter, irresistible march of evolution, reality ever new-born; you who, by constantly shattering our mental categories, force us to go ever further and further in our pursuit of the truth.

Blessed be you, universal matter, immeasurable time, boundless ether, triple abyss of stars and atoms and generations: you who by overflowing and dissolving our narrow standards of measurement reveal to us the dimensions of God.

Teilhard de Chardin, 'Hymn to Matter'

From the cowardice that dare not face new truth
From the laziness that is content with half truth
From the arrogance that thinks it knows all truth,
Good Lord, deliver me.

A Prayer from Kenya

God give me work
Till my life shall end
And life
Till my work is done
*On the grave of
Winifred Holtby,
novelist* (1898–1935)

O Lord, our Saviour, who hast warned us that thou wilt require much of those to whom much is given, grant that we, whose lot is cast in so goodly a heritage, may strive together the more abundantly by prayer, by almsgiving, by fasting, and by every other appointed means, to extend to others what we so richly enjoy; and as we have entered into the labour of other men, so to labour that in their turn other men may enter into ours, to the fulfilment of thy holy will, and our own everlasting salvation; through Jesus Christ our Lord.

St Augustine (354–430)

I asked for strength that I might achieve;
I was made weak that I might learn humbly to obey.

I asked for health that I might do greater things;
I was given infirmity that I might do better things.

I asked for riches that I might be happy;
I was given poverty that I might be wise.

I asked for power that I might have the praise of
    men;
I was given weakness that I might feel the need of
    God.

I asked for all things that I might enjoy life;
I was given life that I might enjoy all things.

I got nothing that I had asked for,
but everything that I had hoped for.

Almost despite myself my unspoken prayers were
    answered;
I am among all men, most richly blessed.

Unknown Confederate soldier.

Eternal Father,
source of life and light,
whose love extends to all people,
all creatures, all things:
Grant us that reverence for life
which becomes those who believe in you;
lest we despise it, degrade it,
or come callously to destroy it.
Rather let us save it,
secure it, and sanctify it,
after the example of your Son,
Jesus Christ our Lord.

Robert Runcie

Be present, O merciful God, and protect us through
the silent hours of this night, so that we who are
wearied by the changes and chances of this fleeting
world may rest upon thy eternal changelessness;
through Jesus Christ our Lord.

The Office of Compline

I am serene because I know thou lovest me.
Because thou lovest me, naught can move me from my peace.
Because thou lovest me, I am as one to whom all good has
come.

Alistair Maclean, Hebridean Altars

Also by David Adam
and published by

THE EDGE OF GLORY
Prayers in the Celtic Tradition

'It is a style that beautifully combines God's glory with
everyday events, Containing prayers for individual
devotions and corporate worship, they all express joyful
faith in God.'
Christian Family

THE CRY OF THE DEER
Meditations on the Hymn of St Patrick

Takes us deeper into the prayer experience through a
series of meditations leading into practical exercises. They
enable us to affirm the Presence of God and to find in our
faith a vital living relationship which touches every aspect
of our lives.

TIDES AND SEASONS
Modern prayers in the Celtic Tradition

'The thought of these prayers is immediately attractive,
often beautiful, with an incantatory lilt. The book,
decorated with drawings in Celtic style, will be gratefully
welcomed.'
Church Times

THE EYE OF THE EAGLE
Meditations on the Hymn 'Be thou my vision'

Explores the varied aspects of vision using a popular hymn
to discover the spiritual riches which are hidden in the
lives of us all.

Also published by

TRi∧NGLE

The PRAYING WITH series, books making accessible the
words of some of the great characters and traditions of
faith for use by all Christians.

PRAYING WITH SAINT AUGUSTINE
Introduction by Murray Watts

PRAYING WITH SAINT FRANCIS
Introduction by David Ford

PRAYING WITH THE NEW TESTAMENT
Introduction by Joyce Huggett

PRAYING WITH SAINT TERESA
Introduction by Elaine Storkey

PRAYING WITH THE JEWISH TRADITION
Introduction by Lionel Blue

PRAYING WITH THE OLD TESTAMENT
Introduction by Richard Holloway

PRAYING WITH THE ORTHODOX TRADITION
Preface by Kallistos Ware

PRAYING WITH THE ENGLISH HYMN WRITERS
Compiled and Introduced by Timothy Dudley-Smith

PRAYING WITH THE ENGLISH MYSTICS
Compiled and Introduced by Jenny Robertson

PRAYING WITH THE ENGLISH TRADITION
Preface by Robert Runcie

PRAYING WITH THE ENGLISH POETS
Compiled and Introduced by Ruth Etchells

PRAYING WITH THE MARTYRS
Preface by Madeleine L'Engle

PRAYING WITH JOHN DONNE AND GEORGE HERBERT
Preface by Richard Harries